SPORTS BIOGRAPHIES

SERENA WILLIAMS

KENNY ABDO

Fly!
An Imprint of Abdo Zoom
abdobooks.com

abdobooks.com

Published by Abdo Zoom, a division of ABDO, P.O. Box 398166, Minneapolis, Minnesota 55439. Copyright © 2023 by Abdo Consulting Group, Inc. International copyrights reserved in all countries. No part of this book may be reproduced in any form without written permission from the publisher. Fly!™ is a trademark and logo of Abdo Zoom.

Printed in the United States of America, North Mankato, Minnesota.
102022
012023

Photo Credits: Alamy, AP Images, Getty Images, iStock, Shutterstock
Production Contributors: Kenny Abdo, Jennie Forsberg, Grace Hansen
Design Contributors: Neil Klinepier

Library of Congress Control Number: 2022937314

Publisher's Cataloging-in-Publication Data

Names: Abdo, Kenny, author.
Title: Serena Williams / by Kenny Abdo
Description: Minneapolis, Minnesota : Abdo Zoom, 2023 | Series: Sports biographies | Includes online resources and index.
Identifiers: ISBN 9781098280284 (lib. bdg.) | ISBN 9781098280819 (ebook) | ISBN 9781098281113 (Read-to-Me ebook)
Subjects: LCSH: Williams, Serena, 1981---Juvenile literature. | Tennis players--United States--Biography--Juvenile literature. | African American women tennis players-Biography--Juvenile literature. | Sports--Biography--Juvenile literature.
Classification: DDC 796.092--dc23

TABLE OF CONTENTS

Serena Williams................ 4

Early Years..................... 8

Going Pro..................... 12

Legacy 18

Glossary 22

Online Resources 23

Index 24

SERENA WILLIAMS

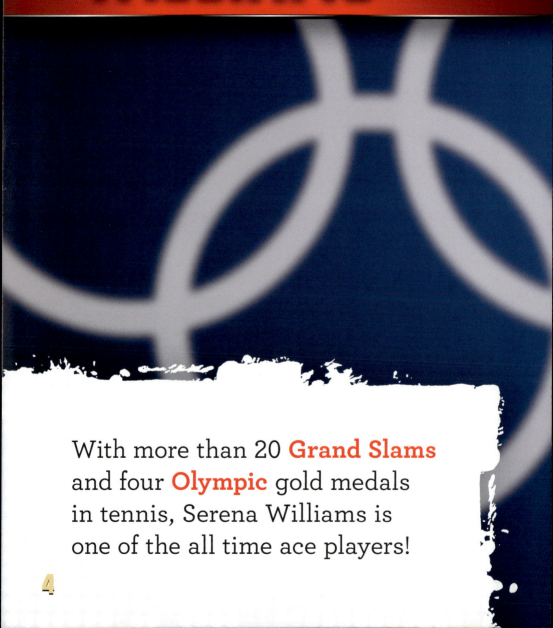

With more than 20 **Grand Slams** and four **Olympic** gold medals in tennis, Serena Williams is one of the all time ace players!

While setting historical records with unmatched talent, Williams is an inspiration to generations of young athletes around the world.

Her skills on the court are so amazing, a type of victory in the game is even named after her!

EARLY YEARS

Serena Jameka Williams was born in Saginaw, Michigan, in 1981. From a very young age, she and her older sister, Venus, were passionate about tennis.

Williams moved with her family to California when she was four. She and her sister Venus were coached and mentored in tennis by their father, Richard Williams.

When Williams was nine, the family moved to Florida. There, she and her sister were coached by Rick Macci.

GOING PRO

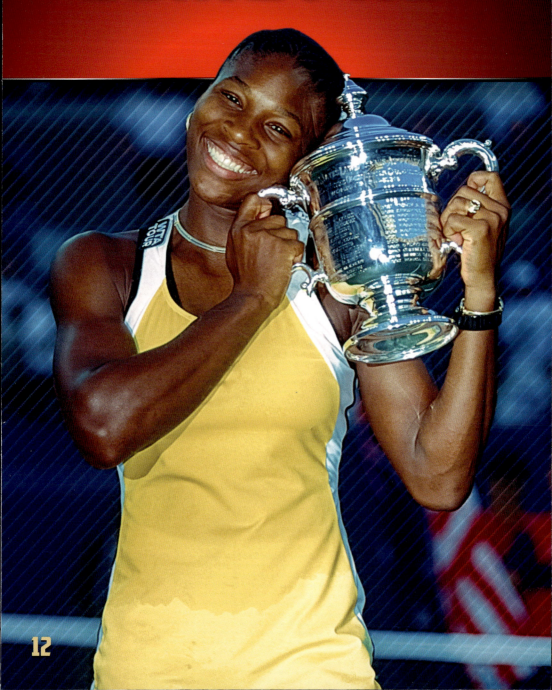

Williams' professional **debut** was in 1995. Winning the U.S. Open at age 17, she **clinched** her first **majors** singles **title**!

Between 2002 and 2003, Williams won four straight **titles** at the French Open, Wimbledon, U.S. Open, and the Australian Open. It was called the **Serena Slam**!

Williams achieved another **Serena Slam** between 2014 and 2015. She became the third person in history to win each **majors** championship more than three times!

Williams won another singles event at the 2020 ASB Classic. She played the 1,000th match of her career at the Italian Open that same year!

In 2021, a leg injury forced Williams to sit out from the US and Australian Opens. She came back in 2022 to give a stunning performance at the US Open! But Williams announced that it would be her last. She made the decision to step away from tennis to focus on other things that were important to her.

LEGACY

Williams works with many charities. She has helped fund and bring new schools to Africa. Williams has been recognized many times for her charity work.

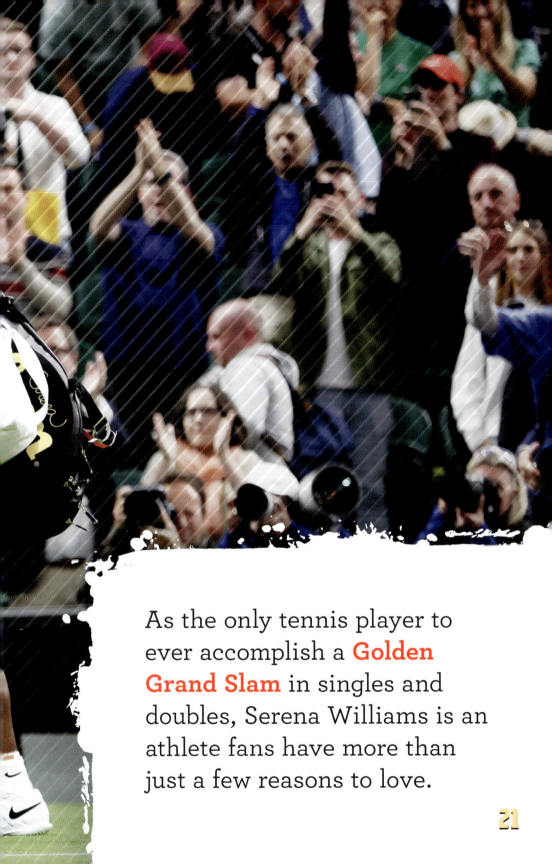

As the only tennis player to ever accomplish a **Golden Grand Slam** in singles and doubles, Serena Williams is an athlete fans have more than just a few reasons to love.

GLOSSARY

clinch – to confirm a win.

debut – a first appearance.

Golden Grand Slam – when a player wins all four Grand Slam tournaments and the Olympic gold medal during their career.

Grand Slam – winning all four major championships in the same calendar year.

majors – the four most important tournaments in tennis. They include the Australian Open, the French Open, Wimbledon, and the US Open.

Olympic Games – the biggest international athletic event held as separate winter and summer competitions every four years in a different city.

Serena Slam – winning all of the major tournaments in a row, but not necessarily all within the same calendar year.

title – a first-place position in a contest.

ONLINE RESOURCES

To learn more about Serena Williams, please visit **abdobooklinks.com** or scan this QR code. These links are routinely monitored and updated to provide the most current information available.

INDEX

ASB Classic 16

California 10

charity 18

Florida 11

injury 17

Italian Open 16

Macci, Rick 11

majors 13, 14, 17

Michigan 9

Olympics 4

records 6, 15, 21

Serena Slam 14, 15

titles 13, 14

Williams, Richard 10

Williams, Venus 9, 10, 11